D1289478

MONSTER
Bulldozers

by Chris Bowman

BELLWETHER MEDIA • MINNEAPOLIS, MN

Note to Librarians, Teachers, and Parents:

Blastoff! Readers are carefully developed by literacy experts and combine standards-based content with developmentally appropriate text.

Level 1 provides the most support through repetition of high-frequency words, light text, predictable sentence patterns, and strong visual support.

Level 2 offers early readers a bit more challenge through varied simple sentences, increased text load, and less repetition of high-frequency words.

Level 3 advances early-fluent readers toward fluency through increased text and concept load, less reliance on visuals, longer sentences, and more literary language.

Level 4 builds reading stamina by providing more text per page, increased use of punctuation, greater variation in sentence patterns, and increasingly challenging vocabulary.

Level 5 encourages children to move from "learning to read" to "reading to learn" by providing even more text, varied writing styles, and less familiar topics.

Whichever book is right for your reader, Blastoff! Readers are the perfect books to build confidence and encourage a love of reading that will last a lifetime!

This edition first published in 2014 by Bellwether Media, Inc.

No part of this publication may be reproduced in whole or in part without written permission of the publisher. For information regarding permission, write to Bellwether Media, Inc., Attention: Permissions Department, 5357 Penn Avenue South, Minneapolis, MN 55419.

Library of Congress Cataloging-in-Publication Data

Bowman, Chris, 1990-
  Monster Bulldozers / by Chris Bowman.
    pages cm – (Blastoff! Readers. Monster Machines)
  Audience: Age 5-8.
  Audience: Grades K to 3.
  Includes bibliographical references and index.
  Summary: "Developed by literacy experts for students in kindergarten through grade three, this book introduces bulldozers to young readers through leveled text and related photos"– Provided by publisher.
  ISBN 978-1-62617-053-7 (hardcover : alk. paper)
  1. Bulldozers–Juvenile literature. I. Title.
  TA725.B64 2014
  629.225–dc23
                    2013035107

Printed in the United States of America, North Mankato, MN.

Table of Contents

Monster Bulldozers!

Big bulldozers help **miners**, builders, and soldiers.

They push
sand, rocks,
and gravel.

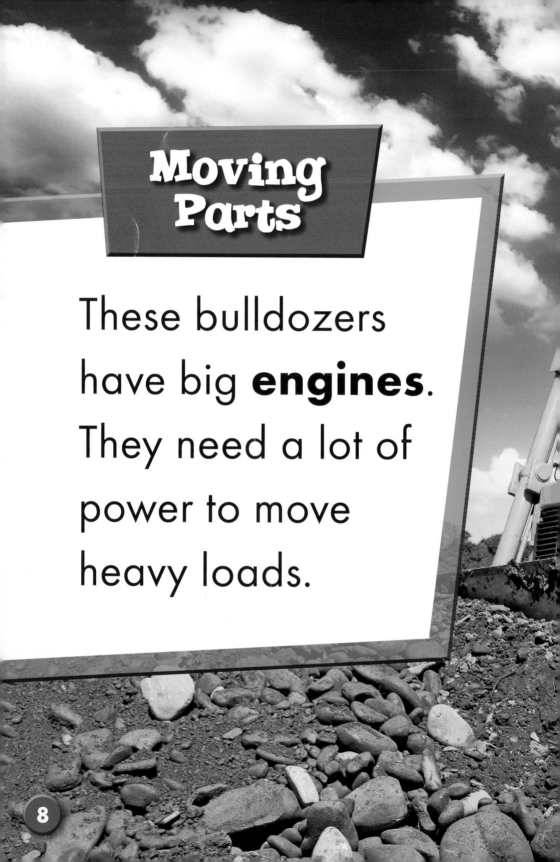

Moving Parts

These bulldozers have big **engines**. They need a lot of power to move heavy loads.

engine

The bulldozers have **rippers** in back. These look like huge claws!

rippers

Rippers break
rocks and hard
ground down
into pieces.

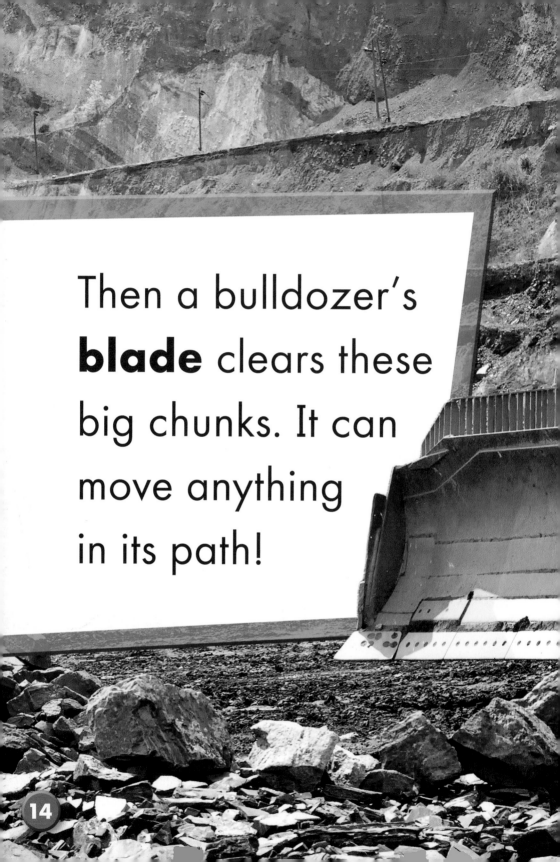

Then a bulldozer's **blade** clears these big chunks. It can move anything in its path!

blade

The ground can be bumpy. Bulldozers have big **tracks** that do not get stuck.

tracks

Military Bulldozers

Soldiers use some big bulldozers in **military zones**. These machines have **armor**.

armor

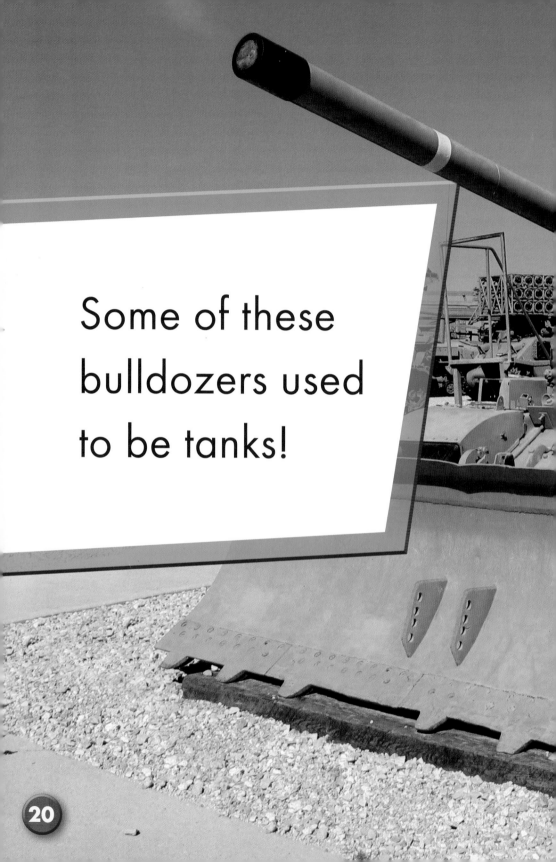

Some of these bulldozers used to be tanks!

Glossary

armor—shields that protect against bullets

blade—a big metal plate that looks like a shovel

engines—machines that power vehicles

military zones—areas where soldiers fight

miners—workers who collect resources from the ground

rippers—sharp tools used to break apart hard objects

tracks—large belts that move over a series of wheels; bulldozers move on tracks.

To Learn More

AT THE LIBRARY

Askew, Amanda. *Bulldozers*. Buffalo, N.Y.: Firefly Books, 2010.

Brady, Peter. *Bulldozers In Action*. Mankato, Minn.: Capstone Press, 2012.

Kawa, Katie. *Bulldozers*. New York, N.Y.: Gareth Stevens Pub., 2012.

ON THE WEB
Learning more about bulldozers is as easy as 1, 2, 3.

1. Go to www.factsurfer.com.

2. Enter "bulldozers" into the search box.

3. Click the "Surf" button and you will see a list of related Web sites.

With factsurfer.com, finding more information is just a click away.

Index

The images in this book are reproduced through the courtesy of: bondgrunge, front cover, pp. 14-15; Stephen McSweeny, pp. 4-5; kaband, pp. 6-7; risteski goce, pp. 8-9, 10-11; We Shoot/ Alamy, p. 9 (small); abutyrin, pp. 12-13; stoonn, pp. 16-17; Asaf Eliason, pp. 18-19; Buckvoed/ Wikipedia, pp. 20-21.